HONOR

URIAH P. LEVY CENTER
AND JEWISH CHAPEL

UNITED STATES NAVAL ACADEMY | BOGGS & PARTNERS ARCHITECTS

SANDOW MEDIA CORPORATION

Produced and published by Sandow Media Corporation, Inc.

Library of Congress Catalog Card Number: 2007907359
ISBN: 978-0-9764713-9-4
First Printing: November 2007
Printed in China
Distributed by Publishers Group West

CEO AND PUBLISHER	ADAM I. SANDOW
MANAGING EDITOR	PAMELA LERNER JACCARINO
CREATIVE DIRECTOR	YOLANDA E. YOH
SENIOR ART DIRECTOR	DARKO MUHL
ART DIRECTORS	PAULA FONTANA, MICHELLE RESTANTE
GRAPHIC DESIGNER	JAMES WEINER
COPY EDITOR	H. SUSAN MANN

S A N D O W | M E D I A ™

Always exceeding expectations.

TELEPHONE 561.750.0151
FAX 561.750.0152
www.sandowmedia.com

Sandow Media Corporation is a cutting-edge publishing company built around a single philosophy: always exceed expectations. Based in Boca Raton, Florida, Sandow Media Corporation is defined by an unrelenting drive toward quality and innovation. Founded in 2002 by Adam I. Sandow, Sandow Media specializes in developing distinguished consumer books and magazines in the categories of travel, shelter and beauty. Sandow Media builds uniquely positioned publications that thrive both in print and online. Creativity is at the core of every segment of its business, which is clearly evident in all its products and brands.

DEDICATED TO BERYL AND HELEN BOGGS

table of contents

the mission of the United States Naval Academy is to develop midshipmen morally, mentally and physically and to imbue them with the highest ideals of duty, honor and loyalty in order to provide graduates who are dedicated to a career of naval service and have potential for future development in mind and character to assume the highest responsibilities of command, citizenship and government

COMMODORE URIAH P LEVY
CENTER

FOREWORD

The mission of the United States Naval Academy is to develop midshipmen morally, mentally and physically into combat leaders of character for our Navy and Marine Corps. It is not by accident that moral development is listed first in our mission. We want our graduates to understand and demonstrate strong leadership, unassailable personal integrity, high ethical values and outstanding character.

Spiritual growth can be an important part of that moral development for those who so believe. Whether Roman Catholic, Protestant, Latter-day Saint, Jewish, Muslim, Hindu or one of the many other religious faiths in our national mosaic, we owe our midshipmen the opportunity to practice their beliefs, as well as to understand how religion enters into their role as combat leaders. The Commodore Uriah P. Levy Center and Jewish Chapel provides a critical addition in our efforts to strengthen individual midshipman faith while teaching understanding and tolerance for the beliefs of others.

Furthermore, it is our hope that this beautiful building will help our midshipmen take honor and values and character into their very souls, and enable great strides in fulfilling Commodore Uriah P. Levy's dream of establishing the practical balance between personal spiritual development and professional moral behavior.

RODNEY P. REMPT
VICE ADMIRAL, UNITED STATES NAVY
SUPERINTENDENT, UNITED STATES NAVAL ACADEMY

Ernest Flagg (1857-1947) was commissioned by the United States Naval Academy in 1895 to design a "new" Naval Academy to replace a mélange of 19th-century buildings often criticized as outdated and inadequate. An American-born architect, Flagg was a student of the venerable École des Beaux-Arts in Paris, France, an institution attended by many of America's greatest architects of the time. The Beaux Arts design Flagg imparted on the Naval Academy was also the style of choice he used for his other prominent works, including the State Capitol at Olympia, Washington; the Corcoran Gallery of Art in Washington, D.C.; and the Singer Tower in New York City, which at that time established a new record for its height. A champion of the "modern" French school of architecture and a former president of the New York Society of Beaux-Arts Architects, Flagg was one of the most innovative practitioners of the Beaux Arts movement in America.

The Beaux Arts style primarily influenced U.S. architecture a few decades before and after the turn of the 20th century and was especially inspired by the 1893 World's Columbian Exposition held in Chicago. The style frequently dictated grand public and institutional buildings, and can prominently be seen in the stately private homes of America's industrial barons of that era. The celebrated Beaux Arts architectural style emphasized classical Greco-Roman forms and styles, as well as a revival of rich decoration, elaborate detailing and formal planning.

Flagg followed the Beaux Arts rigid compositional method for his design of the Naval Academy site and buildings. Firmly based in Classical tenets of architecture, systems of symmetry, proportion, repetition and hierarchy, with strong connections between plan and elevation, were generously applied.

In May 1898, Congress appropriated $500,000 to start rebuilding the entire school according to Flagg's plan. His design swiftly transformed the campus from its poorly built, unsafe and inconveniently located state, not entirely pleasing to the eye, into what would become part of the "new" Annapolis. Starting with the replacement of the unsightly and ancient Main Quarters and Annexes, construction began on the "New Academy's" first building, the Armory, later named Dahlgren Hall. Over the next decade, with additional appropriations of approximately $8 million, the Armory was completed, along with a chapel; Bancroft Hall and its exquisite Center Section Recreation and Memorial halls; MacDonough, Maury, Sampson, and Mahan halls; the Administration building; the Superintendent's (later named Buchanan) House; the Officers and Faculty Club; and more new buildings all built in the Beaux Arts style. These grandiose structures represent an important era of progress in built form for the United States Naval Academy, and they are distinguished by their monumental columns, grand stairways, large arched openings, variety of stone finishes, entablatures topped with balustrades and tall parapets, pronounced cornices, projections of decorative features, and exuberant details.

URIAH PHILLIPS LEVY

Uriah Phillips Levy (1792–1862) holds an esteemed place in American history. With a Renaissance persona, he journeyed through life championing human rights, the Navy, Judaism and architecture. In addition to being a passionate seaman and ardent patriot, Levy was a courageous hero, a pioneer of humanism and historic preservation, and a successful entrepreneur who always took great pride in his heritage.

Born April 22, 1792, into a distinguished Jewish family of Philadelphia patriots, Uriah Levy was profoundly influenced by his maternal grandfather, Jonas Phillips, who served as his mentor in combining lifelong patriotism, religious devotion and admiration for Thomas Jefferson. At the tender age of 10, Uriah Levy began his naval career by running away from home to become a cabin boy aboard the trading ship *New Jerusalem*. His vast knowledge of ships and sailing grew as a seaman aboard ships owned by John Coulter, a leading Philadelphia merchant trader and family friend. Within a decade, Levy quickly rose from apprentice seaman to captain and part owner of a schooner.

At the onset of the War of 1812, Levy volunteered and was assigned to the *Argus*, and later was appointed acting lieutenant. He and the crew were subsequently captured by the British and imprisoned in England for the duration of the war. During the next fifty years, Levy faced religious persecution from many fellow naval officers and endured six courts-martial, all related to anti-Semitism. Throughout his life, he continued to defend and uphold his religious beliefs, along with other just and honorable causes he would embrace and champion. Foremost among these causes are the following.

Humanism: Levy actively campaigned to end the practice of flogging as a form of punishment. His proudest achievement was thus recorded on his tombstone. It reads "Father of the law for the abolition of the barbarous practice of corporal punishment in the United States Navy."

Preservation: In mid-career, after having invested successfully in New York City real estate, Levy was able to manifest his admiration for Thomas Jefferson by being the benefactor of many symbolic testimonials. In 1836, Levy purchased Thomas Jefferson's estate, Monticello, in Virginia and began its arduous restoration and preservation; in his will, he bequeathed Monticello "to the people of the United States." Monticello remained in the Levy family until it was purchased by the Jefferson Memorial Foundation in 1923.

Patriotism: Levy was appointed lieutenant by President James Monroe in 1817, and to commander by President Andrew Jackson in 1837. In 1844, President John Tyler appointed him captain. In 1860, Levy was entrusted with the command of the entire Mediterranean Fleet and became its flag officer. Elevated to the Navy's highest rank, Commodore Levy was the first Jewish American in the United States Navy to attain a rank equivalent to admiral. At the start of the Civil War, President Abraham Lincoln installed him on the Courts-Martial Board in Washington.

Uriah P. Levy fervently served his country until his death on March 22, 1862. He is buried in Brooklyn, New York.

JEWISH NAVAL HERO

Long before the Dreyfus Affair—the legendary anti-Semitic trials for treason of a French military officer at the turn of the 20th century that resulted in his wrongful conviction and sentencing to Devil's Island before being fully exonerated—an American naval officer faced similar adversities. Throughout his career, Uriah P. Levy was a victim of ruthless and relentless anti-Semitism, on land and at sea.

Levy's first encounter with anti-Semitism in the Navy took place while serving as a sailing master aboard the *Franklin* in 1816. Insulted by Lieutenant William Potter, a drunken anti-Semitic officer, Levy retaliated and was challenged by him to a duel. After initially refusing, Levy defended his honor, fought and killed Potter and was indicted by a grand jury. Though Levy was subsequently acquitted, it was to be his destiny to have to defend his conduct, his good name and his religion. Over the next twenty-five years, he would face six naval courts-martial. The charges—disobedience, contempt, scandalous and ungentlemanly conduct, lying, cowardice, using provoking and reproachful words—were frequently fabricated and unfounded, and many of his sentences were ultimately mitigated or disapproved.

While in command of the U.S.S. *Vandalia* in 1838, Levy saw an opportunity to establish new rules and regulations for sailor conduct and discipline by doing away with the lash. His reforms were not well received and resulted in his sixth and final court-martial in 1842. Uriah Levy was dismissed from the Navy, and there was no doubt that he was yet again a victim of prejudice. Levy was astounded when, a short time later, President Tyler reversed the court's verdict and further recommended that Levy be promoted to captain. Nevertheless, during the fifteen years following Levy's reinstatement, each of his applications for a command were repeatedly denied, despite his offer to devote his pay to charity, which was ignored.

Levy's public record is extraordinary in spite of the accusations made against him and the unconscionable treatment he suffered. Prejudice also pervaded his nonmilitary public life, where his generosity of good will and patriotism were repeatedly rebuffed. Persistent assaults were made on his character, including recurring accusations of greed, selfishness and lack of patriotism, for many years after he had purchased and restored Monticello. The statue of Thomas Jefferson prominently displayed in the United States Capitol was donated by Levy to the United States in 1834 but was not formally acknowledged until forty years later. When the Thomas Jefferson Foundation purchased Monticello in 1923, every trace of the Levy family and its preservation role was removed. Just as it took the French army more than a century to admit publicly that it had been wrong in the Dreyfus Affair, it was not until 1985, one hundred and forty-nine years after Uriah Levy's original purchase, that the Foundation officially recognized the Levy family.

Prevailing against anti-Semitism throughout his career was a testament of Uriah Levy's admiration for Thomas Jefferson, especially Jefferson's ideas on religious freedom. In an 1833 letter, Levy acclaimed, "Jefferson serves as an inspiration to millions of Americans. He did much to mold our Republic in a form in which a man's religion does not make him ineligible for political or governmental life." Inarguably, this doctrine inspired and served the exceptional life of Uriah Levy.

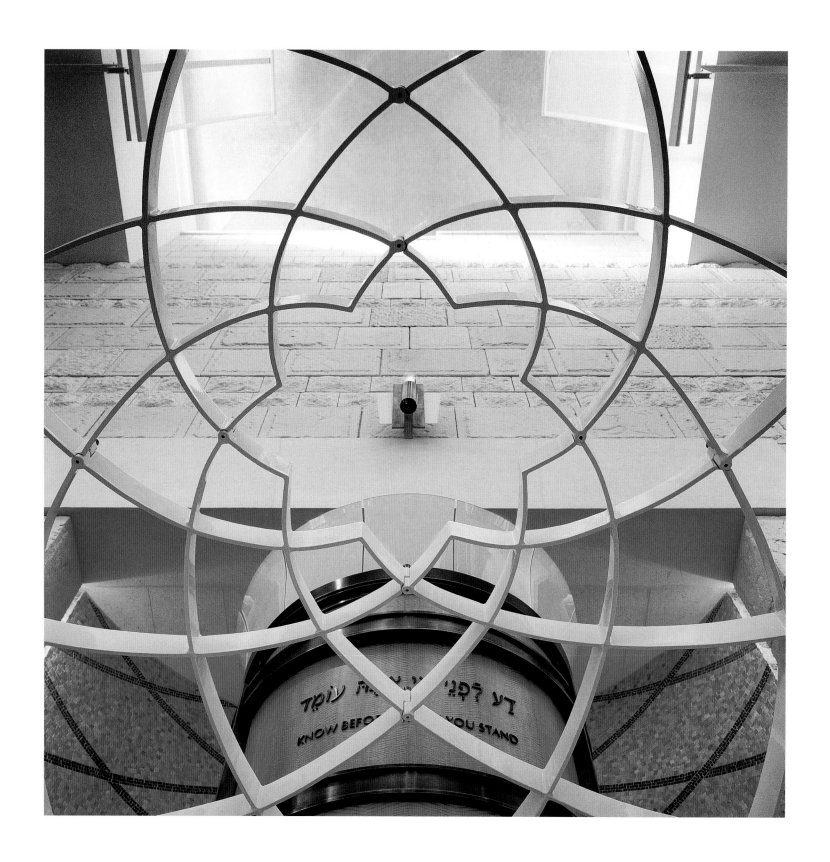

SACRED SPACE

Boggs & Partners Architects of Annapolis, Maryland, under the design lead of Joseph Boggs, FAIA, was selected by the Friends of the Jewish Chapel to design the Uriah P. Levy Center and Jewish Chapel, similar to how Ernest Flagg was chosen as the architect to design the "new" Naval Academy at the turn of the twentieth century. Both architects represent high art and technology with a "modern" sense of style and the courage to embrace change.

Respectful of both the Naval Academy and history, Joseph Boggs created the Levy Center as a new landmark to enhance the prominence of the naval institution while subtly reflecting the original Beaux Arts style designed by Ernest Flagg. Boggs' design for the Center and Chapel embodies intellectual and emotional engagement and the art of architecture. Delineating the entry court, the Center's gardens offer the opportunity for reflection. They begin and end the building with ceremony and formality and mirror the spirituality found inside. The 35,000-square-foot structure includes the rotunda; the Jewish Chapel, which comprises the entire east wing; and the Uriah P. Levy Center in its west wing. Using classical symmetry, the building serves as a collector and epicenter axis for midshipmen circulating to Mitscher Hall, a primary place for social and cultural activities, and toward Farragut Field and Chesapeake Bay. As well, it serves as a symbolic intersection that takes them east and west to their living quarters in Bancroft Hall.

The entry rotunda sets an introductory tone, welcoming visitors from every direction in the tenor of Uriah Levy's principles, and it recalls his admiration for Thomas Jefferson: The pavilion is of classical octagonal form, the geometry Thomas Jefferson used in his design of Monticello, in Virginia. The rotunda is deliberately imageless except for selectively chosen detail. Deeply recessed Stars of David rest protected in each of the rotunda's eight openings. The Jerusalem mosaic stone dome and the planter recall nature and life, and the enclosure itself resonates strength and resolve.

The Levy Center and Jewish Chapel is a denominational building that is equally nondenominational and meant to appeal to all midshipmen. The complex is a classic building of modern Beaux Arts beauty and order, and an ethereal building of space and natural light. The surfaces and connections breathe undertones of astute detail throughout. Centrally located off the rotunda, the three-story Jewish Chapel soars in both spiritual height and intimacy in the overhead mezzanine. Within the Chapel, more-overt symbolism lies in the spectacular Jerusalem stone altar wall surround of the traditionally inspired *bimah*, holy Ark and *ner tamid*. In the main atrium, a Wall of Honor displays the name of each donor engraved on a block of Jerusalem stone. The west wing includes social spaces and the library, where midshipmen of all faiths meet and study, helping to guide them as officers and national leaders for generations to come.

INTO THE REALM

Any new building that was honored to be placed here needed to

EMBRACE ERNEST FLAGG'S BEAUX ARTS ARCHITECTURE

The United States Naval Academy is steeped in tradition, respect and history. With these values in mind, the design for the Levy Center and Chapel took shape. The site selected is the area framed by Mitscher Hall, Farragut Field and Bancroft Hall. The historic Bancroft Hall Courtyard, facing south toward the Chesapeake Bay, demanded a respectful architectural solution. The scale and physical proportions needed to be appropriate, signaling inclusion and an open invitation to all.

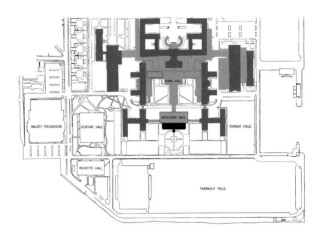

site selection

The vast granite expanses of Bancroft Hall rise behind and on either side of the Levy Center. The Hall's extensive wings wrap around the sacred structure in a seeming embrace. The Levy Center and Chapel stands purposefully at this natural crossroads, adjacent to midshipmen living quarters and the main dining facility, King Hall. It is significant that the spot chosen is enveloped by Bancroft Hall, where midshipmen live, as this is in line with the academy's mission: to develop midshipmen morally, mentally and physically.

The Levy Center defers to the existing architecture surrounding the site. The façade reflects a study of historical references by the architect. The heavily rusticated granite stone and copper roofs of Bancroft and Mitscher halls are eloquently translated in the Levy Center structure. The first two levels of the Center's southern façade respect and draw from the Mitscher Hall design, and the upper section begins to rise from these two-tiered sections with the rustication of stone and gently arched windows.

historical reference

proverbial reach

The rising mass, indicated by a series of deeply punched square windows, appears to lift out of the traditional forms. A modern cantilevered cornice flares out at the top, leading the eye up toward the sky while lightening the mass. Both the east and west symmetrical masses similarly have this uplift, signifying a proverbial reach toward a higher ideal, both in the Chapel and the Honor Court.

the french derivative copper roofs cap lifting

volumes, protecting the series of frosted

glass windows beneath the roofs' leading

edge. the roofs gently but firmly cap the

light and energy from below.

OUR VISION WAS TO CREATE AN INTEGRATED LEARNING CENTER

where spiritual and moral development can take place.

HOWARD PINSKEY
PRESIDENT, FRIENDS OF THE JEWISH CHAPEL
USNA CLASS OF 1962

entry court

Pedestrian access reflects the classical symmetry of the formal courtyard leading toward the Levy Center and Chapel. A grove of trees surrounds an existing memorial depicted by a square fountain and granite seating, donated by the USNA Class of 1961. At its center is a large, vertical light gray granite obelisk stone engraved with the words of John F. Kennedy. The soothing acoustical sound made by the fountain's water spray quiets the mind and heartens the spirit.

"It is my hope that this Center will become integral to the very core of the Naval Academy. Here, as our country's future leaders, midshipmen of all faiths will set the tone for religious understanding and tolerance as they learn about the Jewish religion and its rich cultural heritage."

HARVEY STEIN
PROJECT FOUNDER

HEAVEN AND EARTH

BE STRONG AND OF COURAGE,

DO NOT BE AFRAID OR DISCOURAGED,

FOR THE LORD YOUR GOD

IS WITH YOU FOREVER.

JOSHUA 1:9

The design of the entrance pavilion pays homage to Thomas Jefferson and the admiration that Uriah P. Levy had for him. Levy fervently admired Jefferson for his steadfast belief in religious freedom and tolerance; in 1836, Levy purchased Jefferson's Monticello estate and restored it to perpetuate Jefferson's legacy. The Levy Center's octagonal pavilion structure is respectful of the primary form seen in Monticello, designed by Thomas Jefferson.

inclusion

The eight sides of the entrance pavilion evoke Jewish symbolism, too, specifically Abraham's multisided tent, which was open in all directions as a sign of greeting. This sense of inclusion and openness encourages a spirit of conviviality. The structure invites visitors in from every direction, allowing all to be welcome, regardless of their faith.

Stepping inside the entrance pavilion, visitors experience the structure's strength and resolve interpreted in a classical architectural language. A domed ceiling of spiraling mosaics draws the eye toward the oculus, with its dramatic view of the sky. The mosaic pattern is meant to signify reaching toward the heavenly realm and is intended to lift the spirit prior to entering the adjoining Berlin Atrium Hall. The plants within the circular planter add continual color. Its stone surround provides a seat for contemplation.

entrance pavilion

clear glass entry doors extend from the

classical form of the pavilion, creating a

transparent vestibule. the glass is softly

obscured to allow a more diffuse and

contemplative entrance into the berlin

atrium hall, which leads into the fellowship

hall and the chapel. light illuminates and

sparkles in the vestibule, suggesting a

mystical experience.

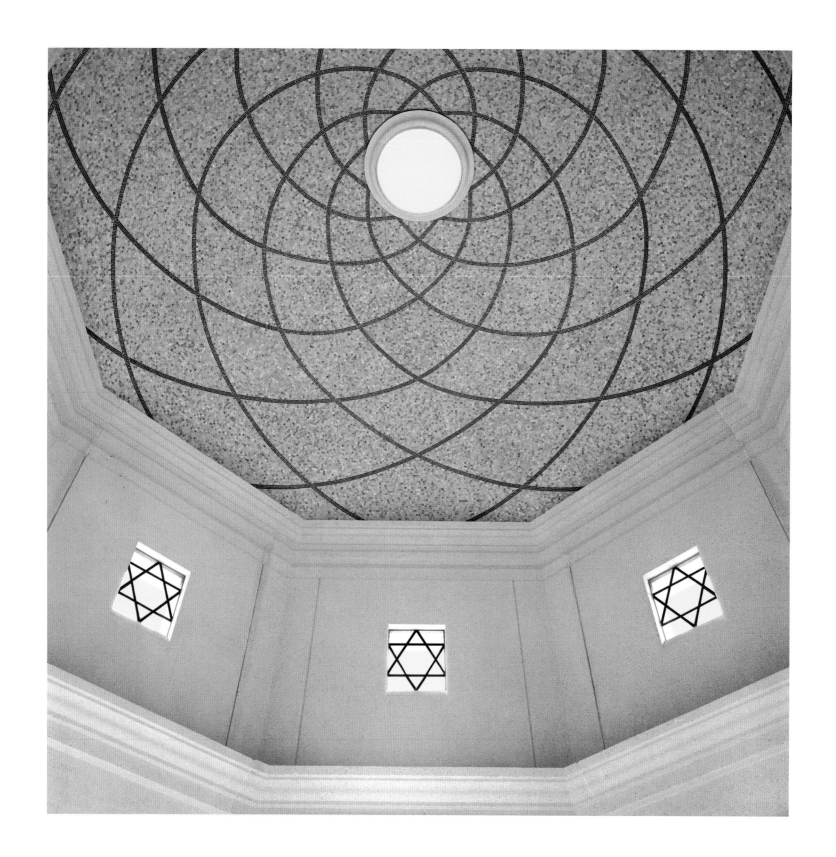

heavenly realm

The entrance pavilion's skylight oculus illuminates the dome's helical pattern and is surrounded by mosaic tiles in shades of red, gray, gold and bone that were quarried in Israel. The design is a double spiral, one of the most complex mosaic patterns to construct. One set of spirals is drawn from each of the eight sides of the pavilion. The spirals were laid in the same manner as mosaics have been set throughout the ages around the world. The lines of the spirals are achieved by the infill stones. Each tile piece was tumbled, to age the surface, and then broken, giving the dome an Old World appearance.

Fittingly, Stars of David grace the classic portico of the building. These deeply recessed bronze Stars of David rest in each of the eight facets above the entry points, signifying a reaching out in all directions. Distant views of the Chesapeake Bay can be seen through the Stars; and as stars have guided midshipmen upon the waters, these Stars of David also are a symbol of direction and of welcoming. Through the stars, nighttime lighting produces a radiance from within, and the pavilion shines as a beacon, beckoning all to enter.

stars of david

THIS INSPIRING SPACE WILL SENSITIZE THE SOULS

of people of all faiths and all religions.

HARVEY STEIN
PROJECT FOUNDER

Beyond the entrance vestibule lies a dramatic space with a floor of precisely laid Jerusalem stone. A bridge, detailed with clear curved glass, softly projects toward the building's entrance. The atrium contains two stone portals, facing east and west, centered under the bridge. To the west is Fellowship Hall, seen through a clear glass wall that allows visitors to view the encased Uriah P. Levy statue beyond the doors, at the end of the barrel vault ceiling. To the east is a glass-enclosed vestibule protecting the Chapel's large wood-and-metal doors.

ESTHER AND WILLIAM MILLER CHAPEL

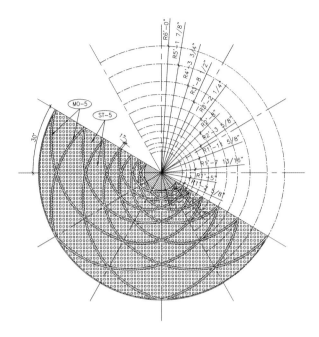

Centered on the stone floor of the Berlin Atrium is a mosaic medallion inlay with a spiral arrangement similar to the mosaic pattern in the entrance pavilion. This pattern lies directly under the conical curved glass bridge circular opening and is illuminated by the atrium's circular skylight. The floor recalls the ancient decorative mosaic floors of Masada, the desert fortress overlooking the Dead Sea in Israel, which inspired the architect. The light falling on the mosaic floor pattern on the ground represents the earthly realm of spiritual energy.

earthly realm

monumental stairway

A glass and stone stairway leads to the bridge above, on the second level, where the Chapel balcony and USNA Conference Center are located. The stairway, which gently rises in a curve from the center of the Berlin Atrium, is designed with a stone base that ascends from the floor to receive the stair's floating stone treads. The airy stairway is intended to be transparent, to maintain a sense of openness and allow light to filter deep into the building.

a translucent prismatic skylight faceted
as a three-dimensional star of david is
situated high above the center of the
atrium. it twinkles with brilliant light
streaming through.

walls of honor

Walls of honor on each side of the Berlin Atrium acknowledge the individuals who made the Levy Center and Chapel a reality. Vertical stacks of stone slabs rise from a heavy stone wainscot. Each stone is engraved and set into a slot in the wood wall. Stainless steel and aluminum add sparkle, enhancing the warmth of the wood. The stacks of stone allow for recognition of donors past and future. The naming wall becomes a soft texture that respectfully places the donors' names, making a pattern of many.

N DREAM.

CT THUS SHALL

EN" PSALM 15:5

Y FOUNDATION

ENSTEIN

FENSTEIN

THE HARRY AND JEANETTE

WEINBERG FOUNDATION, INC.

* * * * *

ROBERTA & MEL FISHER, USNA '55

AND FAMILY

* * *

ERED BY

FOR THE BENEFIT

OF JEWISH MIDSHIPMEN,

FAMILIES AND FRIENDS

OF ALL MIDSHIPMEN

AND ALL WHO VISIT

THE NAVAL ACADEMY

HOWARD R. AND JOY M. BERLIN

DEDICATED BY

CDR HOWARD R. BERLIN,

SUPPLY CORPS, USNR (RET.)

AND HIS FAMILY

WITH DIVERSITY AS

OUR BIRTHRIGHT

AND TOLERANCE OUR GOAL

THE POSSESSION OF BOTH

IS OUR BLESSING...

THE ATTAINMENT, OUR DUTY

VISION AND COURAGE

WITH DEDICATION AND PURPOSE

MADE THIS DREAM A REALITY

* * *

HARVEY & JAN STEIN

AND FAMILY

FRIENDS OF FRED STEN

THE FRIENDS OF FRED STEN

HONORED TO SUPPORT THE

URIAH P. LEVY CENTER AND

JEWISH CHAPEL

UNITED STATES NAVAL ACADEMY

PAST - PRESENT - FUTURE

ALUMNI

"The Levy Center and Chapel makes a statement to the world-wide Jewish community that we, as Jews, are thought of as equals in terms of the military world. No longer will Jewish midshipmen feel in any way, shape or form different from anyone else. This is a long-standing monument to what the Navy encourages."

MEL FISHER
BOARD MEMBER AND CAMPAIGN CHAIR
FRIENDS OF THE JEWISH CHAPEL

SPIRITUAL REALM

THEY THAT GO DOWN
TO THE SEA IN SHIPS,
THAT DO BUSINESS IN GREAT WATERS;
THESE SEE THE WORKS OF THE LORD,
AND HIS WONDERS IN THE DEEP.

PSALM 107:23-24

The Esther and William Miller Chapel is designed as a space of lightness, of memory and of uplifting. The 425-seat Chapel is graced with few religious and architectural elements. Religious decorative icons were purposefully kept subdued, with the intention of allowing all who enter to feel welcome and inspired.

ESTHER AND WILLIAM MILLER CHAPEL

The weighty detail of the substantial wood entry doors imparts a sense of permanence and solidity suitable for the reverence expected when entering a sacred space. Beyond the Chapel entrance are biblical and inspirational passages, both in Hebrew and English, etched into curved panes of backlit glass, which give an ethereal impression. In the anteroom, a Torah recovered from the Holocaust and donated to the Naval Academy is on display. Because it was defiled, this Torah can no longer be used for prayer services. It stands as a source of reflection and remembrance of Jews and others who suffered.

Past the anteroom, the Chapel comes into full view. The vertically oriented space, framed in metal, stone and wood, is grounded by stone mosaic flooring, curved pews and striking white woven metal scrims. The massive, nearly 40-foot-high hand-carved Jerusalem stone wall, inspired by the Western Wall in Jerusalem, stands as a prominent symbol of the Jewish people's rich cultural and religious heritage. Set into the stone wall is an arched recessed mosaic, echoing the spiral motif used elsewhere in the building. It serves as a niche for the holy Ark. White-painted woven stainless-steel scrims run along both sides of the Chapel and upward toward the aluminum-leaf, nearly 47-foot ceiling.

sacred space

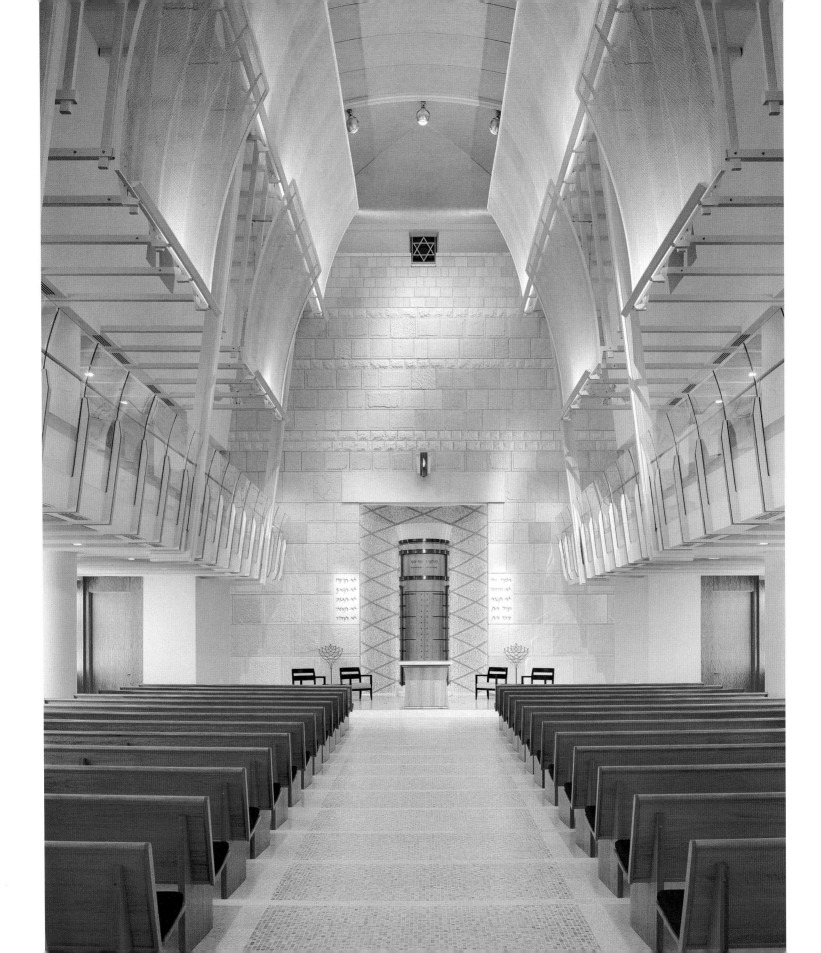

THIS SPACE IS A SYMBOL OF TOLERANCE AND INCLUSION

and for understanding the importance of faith.

RABBI IRVING ELSON
CHAPLAIN, UNITED STATES NAVAL ACADEMY

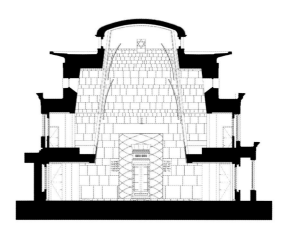

found ruin

The concept of integrating Jerusalem stone into the Chapel was symbolically significant in order to convey a sense of history and to bring a piece of Israel into the sanctuary. The architect traveled to Israel and was inspired by Old Jerusalem, itself a city of walls. The impact of these walls—old and new, reclaimed and rebuilt, dividing and uniting—influenced the Chapel design. The Chapel's Jerusalem stone wall, made from stone of the earth that has been reclaimed through the ages, now serves in this Chapel to remind and to unite.

from ancient to modern

JERUSALEM STONE

Jerusalem's buildings and streets, from humble to majestic, ancient to modern, are built for the most part of stone. The use of this stone has been constant for thousands of years. In order to maintain Jerusalem's striking uniqueness, municipal law established in the early nineteen hundreds mandates the use of Jerusalem stone, which imparts a warm glow of beige hues over the city. The white- and cream-colored Jerusalem stone used in the Chapel was quarried in the hills near Hebron, south of Jerusalem. Especially large stones were chosen, each one varying in size and texture. The appearance of the wall in the Chapel is intended to evoke a sense of history and timelessness—a "found" ruin—as though the architect unearthed an ancient wall and floor, restored it and built a chapel around it.

"The most exciting moment came during my visit to the site. My experience has taught me that as beautiful as the stone is when it is sent off to a site, when one sees it built, there is always a sense of wonder and anticipation. This time it was indescribable. To arrive in Washington, D.C., at the height of the cold, gray winter, and to see a majestic wall radiating light to its surroundings, a light of the Jerusalem hills, made me want to run and put a note between the stones, 'Next Year in Jerusalem.'"

JACOB MORDOCH
OWNER, JERUSALEM GARDENS STONE WORKS

דַּע לִפְנֵי מִי
אַתָּה עוֹמֵד

KNOW BEFORE WHOM YOU STAND

stone tablets

Two large eight-foot stone tablets, hand-carved in Jerusalem with abbreviated versions of the Ten Commandments, are located adjacent to the Ark in the Chapel. The ancient Hebrew font replicates script found in a 4th-century BCE letter from the Nile River Jewish community of Elephantine Island to the High Priest of a temple in Jerusalem. Surprisingly, many of the characters are similar to modern Hebrew script. The purpose of choosing this script, besides its beauty, was to link a historical font to the wall.

aron kodesh

A patterned recessed wall softly surrounds the large cylindrical Ark (*aron kodesh*), the sanctuary's container of Torah scrolls. Designed as a simple wood cylinder, the Ark is handcrafted of anigre wood embellished with bronze banding and a crown of glass. The bronze banding aligns with the stone mosaic in the niche around the Ark, providing a focus for the double helix motif. Bronze buttons adorn the cylinder, adding to the verticality of the piece, which stands as a sentry protecting the sacred texts. The top of the Ark is crowned with twelve pieces of custom curved etched glass. Embraced by the ring of this crown is a wood inlaid Star of David, not visible to the congregation. This inlay is of, and for, the Ark itself, in recognition of its sanctity as a vessel that houses holy texts.

Ner tamid means "eternal light." In every synogague, the *ner tamid* burns quietly while hanging above or near the Ark in remembrance of the Temple in Jerusalem. In the Chapel, the *ner tamid* is set into the stone wall. The flame is a symbol of God's eternal presence in our communities and in our lives, and is never extinguished.

ner tamid

The simple curved pews made of anigre, a highly figured African wood, were placed on a slight radius to promote inclusiveness and to symbolize the radiant energy emanating from the Chapel and reaching out to others. One can best appreciate the space by looking out to the balcony from the *bimah*, which is the raised platform where the Torah is read. Seating in the Chapel faces east, towards Jerusalem.

The floor, made from Jerusalem stone inset with mosaics, was inspired by an ancient mosaic tile floor that was found in the fortress ruins at Masada in Israel. In the Chapel, the main aisle tapers near the *bimah*, with the intention of creating the sense of a sloped floor, to give pause before approaching the Ark.

A *chuppah* is a canopy under which a bride and groom stand during a Jewish wedding ceremony. Handcrafted of white powder coated aluminum, the Chapel's *chuppah* form is based on a double helix, the pattern used throughout the Chapel and elsewhere in the Center to represent the focus of energy from all sources, circling and entwining together, thereby strengthening the whole. When in use, the *chuppah* fits into embeds in the stone floor on the bimah.

Two custom-made bronze menorahs flank the Ark. Their spiral-like double-helix design echoes the continued theme of the heavenly, spiritual and earthly realm, which is carried throughout the Levy Center.

דַּע לִפְנֵי מִי אַתָּה עוֹמֵד

KNOW BEFORE WHOM YOU STAND

"This beautiful building will provide a critical addition in our efforts to strengthen individual midshipmen's faith while teaching understanding of tolerance for the beliefs of others. The Levy Center represents much more than the opportunity to provide a synagogue to meet the long overdue need of a dedicated place of worship for midshipmen of the Jewish faith. It is also an opportunity to invest in the future leadership of our military and of our country. And it fulfills Commodore Levy's dream of establishing a practical balance between personal spiritual development and professional moral behavior."

RODNEY P. REMPT
VICE ADMIRAL, UNITED STATES NAVY
SUPERINTENDENT, UNITED STATES NAVAL ACADEMY

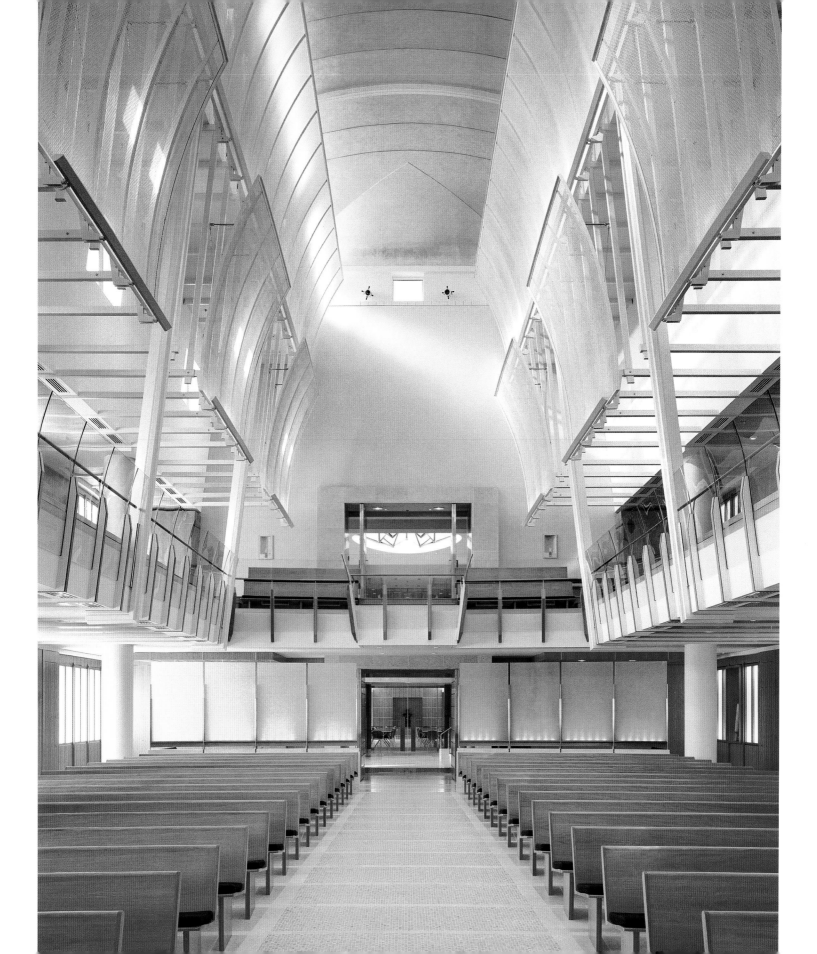

quality of light

The sense of light is an important component of the Chapel's design. Shoji glass, handmade rice paper laminated between two layers of glass, is used on the side walls to allow light to penetrate the space while lending a sense of protection and solitude. Natural unfiltered light enters the Chapel from the east- and west-facing windows. Natural light also comes from above to create dramatic shifts of light within the space and to draw the eye upward.

The sense of upward motion, from the form to the material to the scrims, is significant to the Chapel's design. The scrims' metal supports slope into the base, rising to create an arch. The balcony and curved glass balustrade extend out into the space, floating as if suspended from above.

upward motion

light-filtering scrims, made of woven stainless-steel wire, are suspended with nautical rigging. the scrims help form the view up to the silver-leaf ceiling, which yields a mystical effect. this layered view is designed to lift the spirit.

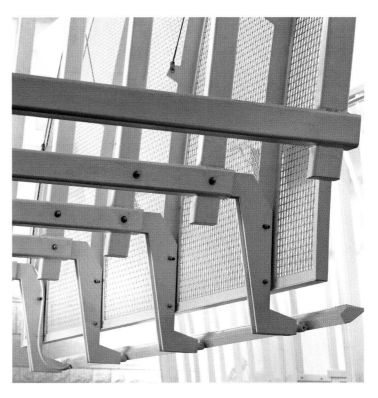

Within the Chapel, the stone used serves to ground physically while the energy from the Ark and pervasive ethereal light serve to provide an emotional lift. It is a space of repose designed to enable midshipmen to prepare to ascend to leadership while guiding them spiritually and morally.

emotional lift

"If Uriah P. Levy were here, I think he would be pleased. I believe he would value the homage we have paid to his mentor, Thomas Jefferson, appreciate the scrims, which resemble sails, and he would see the important connection that this building has with the Academy. We have honored this man of great courage and conviction."

JOSEPH BOGGS
FAIA

EPILOGUE

One of the most difficult things in life is to recognize extraordinary moments as they are happening
and to embrace these precious moments in time.

For me, the realization of this project is one of those moments.

As time has passed since the dedication ceremony of September 17, 2005, and I become further distanced from the intellectual
and emotional challenges that this project presented, the significance of what the Levy Center and Chapel means to me
has changed. What touches me most deeply is not the stone surfaces or the light-filled scrims;
rather, it is the resonance of the spoken word that echoes through the Chapel.

A house of worship cannot speak to the heart without spiritual words, or what I refer to as the "spoken realm." While the Levy Center
and Chapel may inspire the soul as a piece of architecture, it only comes alive as the rabbi speaks within it.

Thousands of years ago when Jews had to relocate, temples were improvised. What made those spaces sacred
was not their architecture but the gravity of the spoken word of a rabbi.

Today, when I reflect on the Chapel, I recall the voice of the rabbi, a voice that truly connects with those who congregate here.
That is as strong as any stone in any wall.

URIAH P. LEVY CENTER AND JEWISH CHAPEL FACTS

LENGTH OF CHAPEL	83'-0"
WIDTH OF CHAPEL	51'-0"
HEIGHT OF CHAPEL CEILING	46'-6"
HEIGHT OF STONE WALL	39'-6"
SEATING CAPACITY	306 First Level
	119 Mezzanine
HEIGHT OF PAVILION DOME	33'-0"
WIDTH OF FACADE	224'-4"
CHAPEL SQ. FT.	4,200 SQ. FT. at First floor
	2,500 SQ. FT. at Mezzanine
	6,700 SQ. FT. Total
TOTAL LEVY CENTER SQ. FT.	32,000 SQ. FT. Levy Center
LEVY CENTER LAYOUT	
FIRST LEVEL	Miller Chapel
	Stein Fellowship Hall
	Jewish Studies Center
	Berlin Atrium
	Weinberg Pavilion
	Ottenstein Grand Lobby
	All Faiths' Chapel
	Laboon Ministry Center
	Midshipmen's Common Student Center
	Mitscher Auditorium (seats 650)
SECOND LEVEL	Character Development Center
	Chaplain Center
THIRD LEVEL	Honor Court
	Ethics Center
STONE SHIPPED FROM ISRAEL	17,724 SQ. FT.
STONE	Hebron White (interior stone)
	Grey Kershaw (exterior stone)
STONE MOSAIC	Benjamin Grey
	Ramon Gold
	Benjamin Gold
	Jerusalem Red
WOOD	Anigre (African hardwood)
GLASS	Low iron glass with rice paper interlayer
CHAPEL CEILING	Aluminum leaf

ARCHITECT	Boggs & Partners Architects
DESIGN TEAM	Joseph A. Boggs, FAIA
	Bonnie K. Johnson
	Anthony DiCamillo
	Robert Holzbach
	Maria Lehman
	Michelle Senneca
CLIENT	Friends of the Jewish Chapel
	Harvey Stein
	Howard Pinskey
OWNER	United States Naval Academy
OWNER'S REPRESENTATIVES	Robert Parsons
	Joseph Rubino
LITURGICAL CONSULTANTS	Rabbi Aaron Landes
	Rabbi Joel Newman
	Rabbi Irv Elson
	Levin/Brown & Associates
PROJECT HISTORIAN	David Hoffberger
CONSULTANT TEAM	
CIVIL ENGINEER/LANDSCAPE	Greenhorne & O'Mara
STRUCTURAL ENGINEER	Cagley & Associates
MEP ENGINEER	GHT Ltd.
CODE CONSULTANT	Rolf Jenson & Associates
ELEVATOR CONSULTANT	Lerch Bates
HARDWARE CONSULTANT	Frank Erbschloe
GEOTECHNICAL ENGINEER	ECS Ltd.
ACOUSTIC DESIGN	Miller, Beam and Paganelli
	RPG
CONSTRUCTION TEAM	
CONSTRUCTION MANAGER	Naval Facilities,
	Washington, D.C. Division
CONTRACTOR	Whiting-Turner Contracting Co.
FPE CONTRACTOR	Shaw-Beneco
QUALITY CONTROL	Sara Henson
INTERIOR SPECIALTIES	
STONEWORK	Rugo Stone (installer)
	Jerusalem Gardens Stone Works (supplier)
GLASS AND METALWORK	Accent Architectural
CUSTOM MILLWORK	Greenbrier Architectural Woodwork
CHAPEL SEATING	New Holland Furniture
ARM METALWORK	Crenshaw Lighting
MESH SCRIMS	Cambridge Architectural
DISPLAY CASES/CHUPPAH	Virginia Metals
ETERNAL LIGHT/FLAME	Sigma Services and Virginia Metals

AWARDS

2006 **Public Building of the Year Award Maryland Society AIA**, state-level professional AIA competition,
with jury of architects and designers from New York State

2006 **Design Honor Award for Interior Architecture** Interfaith Forum on Religion, Art and Architecture (IFRAA),
international-level professional competition with jury of architects, artists and clergy with the goal of honoring the best in
architecture, liturgical design and art for religious spaces

2006 **Design Honor Award for Religious Arts—Ceremonial Object**—Chuppah Interfaith Forum on Religion, Art and Architecture (IFRAA),
national-level professional competition with jury of architects, artists and clergy

2006 **Award for Excellence in Architecture** Northern Virginia AIA Chapter,
regional-level professional AIA competition with jury of peers

2006 **Award for Excellence in Architecture** Chesapeake Bay AIA Chapter,
regional-level professional AIA competition with jury of peers

2006 **Merit Award for Interior Architecture** Washington, D.C. AIA Chapter,
regional-level professional AIA competition with jury of peers

2006 **Merit Award for Government Architecture Best of Year** (B.O.Y. Awards), *Interior Design* magazine,
national-level award juried by *Interior Design* magazine editors and guest critics

2006 **Preservation Award Historic Annapolis Foundation**, local preservation award

2006 **Star Award—Special Award of Merit** for Detail Stone in Architecture—Prism Awards,
international-level professional trade competition to honor outstanding examples of architectural achievement
in the use of natural stone, sponsored by *Architectural Record* magazine and MIA

2006 **Craftsmanship Award for Stonework**, Building Congress & Exchange,
professional trade competition with jury of artisans, contractors and stone professionals,
included a site visit for first-hand review of the level of craftsmanship

2006 **Honorable Mention Award Metal Architecture** Design Awards—Interiors,
professional trade competition with jury of editors of professional metal building journals

2006 **Pinnacle Award for Interiors—Stonework**, Marble Institute of America,
national-level professional trade competition with jury of architects and stone professionals

PUBLICATIONS

"Religious Art & Architecture Awards," by Michael Crosbie, *Faith + Form* magazine, volume XXXIX, number 4

"Best of year: Enjoy the ride," *Interior Design* magazine, December 2006

"A Matter of Faith," by Laura Fischer Kaiser, *Interior Design* magazine, July 2006

"Navy Temple," by William Lebovich, *Architecture Week,* 3 May 2006

"Places of Worship," by John Hughes, *Metalmag,* March/April 2006, volume 7, number 3

"Levy Center and Jewish Chapel: Newest and Brightest Jewel of the Yard," by David Hoffberger, *Shipmate,* November 2005

"Naval Academy Chapel Soars like a Tall Ship," by Benjamin Forgey, *Portland Press Herald,* 29 October 2005

"A Trim Vessel of Worship: Naval Academy's Jewish Chapel Rises to its Challenge," by Benjamin Forgey, *Washington Post,* 23 October 2005

"Levy Center Personifies Moral Strength Through Diversity," by Matt Jarvis, *Trident,* 23 September 2005

"An Anchor for Jewish Midshipmen and Others," by Edward Gunts, *Baltimore Sun,* 18 September 2005

"A ship of their own: Naval Academy opening a Jewish Chapel on campus," by Ira Rifkin, JTA global, 29 August 2005

"A Shrine of Inclusion," by Ira Rifkin, *The Jerusalem Report,* 8 August 2005

"Port of Calling: Creating a Jewish Harbor at the U.S. Naval Academy," by Ira Rifkin, *Baltimore Jewish Times,* 8 July 2005

"Boggs Makes Impact on Annapolis Skyline," Wendi Winters, *The Capital,* 4 April 2004

"Sprirt of Understanding," by Earl Kelly, *The Capital,* 19 September 2003

"Old Salts: Answering to a Higher Calling," *Lifestyles Magazine,* Summer 2001, volume 29, number 174

BOGGS & PARTNERS ARCHITECTS

The innovative design and planning solutions of Boggs & Partners Architects have received international acclaim. The award-winning architectural firm, headquartered in Annapolis, Maryland, brings artistic originality and design excellence to its wide range of corporate, institutional, retail and residential projects. The firm's portfolio demonstrates a growing, developing body of work that continues to intrigue and express. The designs encompass a consistency of quality and purpose at a variety of scales. The work itself is characterized by the careful execution of detail, the formal relationship of parts and the final understanding of form in response to setting. Principal Joseph A. Boggs, FAIA, together with his partners and staff, demonstrates an extraordinary ability to translate strong conceptual approaches into equally compelling architectural forms. The firm's commitment lies in offering expanded services and in providing clients with the necessary resources to maximize real estate assets by planning and designing facilities which support organizational objectives.

This project design was enhanced by the talented efforts of Bonnie K. Johnson, an architect and industrial designer, as well as Anthony Dicamillo, AIA, an industry technical expert who addresses construction detailing and execution. The project took nearly eight years from inception to completion. It required an extraordinary commitment from many professionals involved to make the project a success.

JOSEPH A. BOGGS, FAIA

Through his work in the mid-Atlantic region and abroad, Joseph Boggs has developed a reputation for artistic originality and design excellence in architecture. His thirty-five-year career spans the commercial office, retail, hospitality, interiors and residential arenas. Since the early seventies as a young architectural graduate, Mr. Boggs has distinguished himself as an exemplary designer in a wide range of building types, including corporate, institutional, retail and residential. His ability to determine a strong conceptual base for each project and then translate that concept into three-dimensional architectural forms is a recognized skill. The award-winning work has been widely noted in the national and international architectural press as inventive and original in design solutions and approaches. The majority of his projects are devoid of any context with which to draw from or relate, requiring the architecture to be self-expressing and independent and to spring forth from the landscape of the site. The continual evolution and derivation of contemporary forms throughout his design career is evident in his built work, which numbers over sixty completed projects of different types. His ability to adapt to the scale and programmatic changes that different projects require results in work that is very solid in its approach and execution. Examples of this adaptability are evident in the design of the Filene Center II at Wolf Trap Farm Park; Sallie Mae Headquarters in Reston, Virginia; and the World Headquarters for the Machinists and Aerospace Workers Union in Upper Marlboro, Maryland. These notable achievements represent a growing, developing body of work that continues to intrigue, to be expressive and to promote design as a public experience.

Mr. Boggs is an undergraduate of Virginia Polytechnic Institute & State University with a Master of Architecture from Harvard University Graduate School of Design. The diversity of his work has been the subject of lectures at several universities and he has been the G.T. Ward visiting professor at Virginia Polytechnic Institute & State University. He also has won numerous awards, been published in national and international publications, and was elected to the College of Fellows of the American Institute of Architects in 1995.

SANDOW MEDIA

Sandow Media is a cutting-edge publishing and media company built around a single philosophy: always exceed expectations. Conceived in 2001 by Adam I. Sandow, Sandow Media is defined by an unrelenting focus on quality and creativity. The company's work centers on many sectors of the luxury market, including shelter, beauty and lifestyle. Innovation is at the core of every segment of its business and is evident in all of its products and brands.

Founder Adam Sandow has always believed in the philosophy of giving back, particularly for projects that strike a chord. When the opportunity was presented to the company to underwrite a portion of this book, as well as to concept, write and design it, Mr. Sandow was particularly proud to do so. The story of Uriah Phillips Levy and his courageous battle to fight anti-Semitism moved him, as did the significance of what the Jewish Chapel at the Commodore Uriah P. Levy Center represents. Furthermore, Sandow Media feels privileged to produce a book on the honorable architectural work of Joseph A. Boggs.

ALAN KARCHMER

Alan Karchmer began photographing while studying architecture at Tulane University where he received a Master of Architecture degree in 1978. The foundation of critical architectural thinking that he developed at that time continues to inform his vision. He approaches his work with the perspective of an architect and began his practice in architectural photography immediately upon completion of his studies. For the last twenty years, he has worked in partnership with his wife, photo stylist Sandra Benedum. Her sharp sense of design and perceptive interpretation of color contribute to the clarity and impact of the images. The photographs they create have been widely published in the international architectural press since 1980.

Karchmer and Benedum are called upon by the leading architects of our time to bring their vision and expertise to the representation of architectural designs. The couple are trusted to create the images architects choose to define their work. Karchmer's understanding of the complex motivations and intentions of architecture is paired with a mastery of the craft and art of photography, enabling him to make photographs that are compelling and dynamic, images that bring the viewer into the experience of the place. The artist David Hockney said that our perceptions are formed not by one instantaneous observation but, rather, are composed of hundreds of fragments that the mind synthesizes into a whole. This is the challenge of depicting architecture in a static two-dimensional image. Karchmer's iconic photographs capture a precise moment that suggests the passage of time, a deliberately chosen perspective that implies movement through space, one photograph that distills and reveals a complex series of ideas.

JANET R. WHITE, FAIA

Over the last thirty years, Janet White has held positions and influence that are far-reaching in the practice of architecture and education. In 1977, she began her seventeen-year practice in St. Louis while on the faculty at Washington University. Subsequently, she served as dean of the Hammons School of Architecture in Springfield and on the Missouri Board for Architects and Professional Engineers. She moved to the Washington, D.C. area in 1997 to become the vice president of education for The American Institute of Architects. In 2001, she returned to practice while maintaining active roles in developing the NCARB Prize, an unparalleled practice education award program for the National Council of Architectural Registration Boards, and the first-in-nation accredited Architecture Doctorate program at the University of Hawaii School of Architecture. Currently, she is the design manager for the Embassy Program at KBR in Arlington, Virginia.

A Fellow of The American Institute of Architects, Janet White holds a Master of Architecture and Bachelor of Architecture from the University of Nebraska. In combination with her award-winning practice, she has received honors and grants for exemplary contributions in education and service to the profession. Her projects and programs have been published in professional journals, university press and national news publications. White's passion for architecture, along with Commodore Levy's meaningful history and the elegant detail of the Center and Chapel, inspired her as she wrote the introductory pages to this book.

FRIENDS OF THE JEWISH CHAPEL

Friends of the Jewish Chapel (FOJC), a nonprofit foundation, was formed when a group of Naval Academy graduates along with local and national citizens organized to support the Jewish chaplain at the Naval Academy with efforts to enhance the religious, cultural and social lives of Jewish midshipmen.

In 1996, after recognizing the need for a facility dedicated to Jewish worship and ethics, visionary leaders proposed the creation of the Uriah P. Levy Center and Jewish Chapel. With the approval of the Superintendent of the Naval Academy and the Secretary of the Navy, a national campaign was initiated to raise funds to design, construct and equip this new facility, as well as to establish maintenance and program endowments.

The Uriah P. Levy Center and Jewish Chapel was gifted to the United States Naval Academy. The FOJC will continue to work with the Naval Academy's Jewish chaplain to create and fund educational, religious and cultural programs for the new Center, designed to meet the needs of all midshipmen.

ACKNOWLEDGEMENTS

First, Boggs & Partners Architects would like to thank each and every donor for making this project a reality and for believing in the value that this project represents for future generations of midshipmen and their families as well as the community of Annapolis, Maryland. This project was once just a dream in the mind of Harvey Stein. His vision, coupled with the support and commitment of the Board of Directors of the Friends of the Jewish Chapel and its many members, has resulted in this generous gift to the Naval Academy. We are grateful for the guidance and education of Rabbi Aaron Landes, Rabbi Panitz, Rabbi Newman and Rabbi Elson, who led us through the uncharted territory of designing a Jewish place of worship.

We would also like to acknowledge the United States Naval Academy for its mission for the men and women of the armed forces. Specifically, this project has spanned the tenure of several Superintendents of the Academy, who has each supported the project. Thank you Admiral Larson, Admiral Ryan, Admiral Naughton, Admiral Moore and Admiral Rempt. Support throughout the Naval Academy was led through the dedicated efforts of Captain Robert Parsons. We appreciate the assistance of the personnel in the office of USNA Public Works, the team at Naval Facilities, Washington, D.C., and the office of the Resident Officer in Charge of Construction and the specific effort of Joseph Rubino. Construction was administered by Whiting-Turner Contracting together with the efforts of their many subcontractors and fabricators. We are indebted to Jacob Mordoch of Jerusalem Gardens Stone Works for hosting us during our visit to Israel and the team at Rugo Stone for their exemplary craftsmanship. We thank the custom furniture contractor Shaw-Beneco and applaud the craftsmanship of their fabricators, in particular Greenbrier Architectural Woodworking and Virgina Metals. Much appreciation is also due to our team of consultants at Cagley & Associates, Greenhorne and O'Mara, GHT, ECS, Frank Erbschloe, Miller Beam & Paganelli, Lerch Bates, RJA and RPJ Inc. There are many individuals responsible for contributions to the success of this project. We thank each of you.

We are grateful to Vice Admiral Rodney Rempt for his contribution to this book's foreword and for the exuberant grand opening of the building. Thank you to the Latta Family, Friends of the Jewish Chapel and the Naval Academy Public Affairs Office for supporting the publication of this book.

We appreciate the tremendous team at Sandow Media, who creatively designed, wrote and published this book. Thank you to Adam I. Sandow, who had the foresight and desire to publish a book about this important project, to Mike Ruskin for overseeing the publishing logistics, to Yolanda Yoh for her creative vision, to Pamela Jaccarino for her eloquent words, and to Darko Muhl for his elegant, powerful design. We are inspired by the visual commentary and expression of the project as seen through the photographs of Alan Karchmer. We are grateful for the research, critique and commentary by Janet White, FAIA, who wrote the introductory pages. Thank you each for sharing your perception and interpretation of the work in the pages of this book.

CREDITS

ARCHITECTS

Joseph A. Boggs, FAIA

Bonnie K. Johnson

Anthony DiCamillo

Maria Lorena Lehman

Robert Holzbach

Michelle Senneca

STRUCTURAL ENGINEER

Cagley & Associates

MEP ENGINEER

GHT, Ltd.

CIVIL ENGINEER

Greenhorne & O'Mara

GENERAL CONTRACTORS

Whiting-Turner Contracting Co.

Shaw-Beneco

The following agencies and organizations provided research details and validation of material:

American Jewish Historical Society, New York

National Trust for Historic Preservation, Resource Center, Washington, D.C.

United States Library of Congress, Digital Reference, Washington, D.C.